Ashby de la Zouch Castle and Kirby Muxloe Castle

John Goodall

Introduction

The castles of Ashby de la Zouch and Kirby Muxloe were the creation of William, Lord Hastings, one of the outstanding political figures and artistic patrons of the 15th century. In 1474 Hastings was licensed by Edward IV to fortify these two sites in the Midlands, the heartland of his political power.

At Ashby de la Zouch he adapted an existing manor house. He also built a new chapel, and two towers that still dominate the ruins. One of these contains the remains of a kitchen and the other – the great tower – a complete suite of domestic apartments. Kirby Muxloe was a courtyard residence laid out on a rectangular plan within a moat. Its walls and towers were built of brick laid with decorative patterns.

Lord Hastings was executed in 1483 and work to both castles was interrupted. The unfinished buildings at Kirby were later abandoned but Ashby became the principal seat of his descendants.

During the Civil War, Ashby was an important royalist base under the command of Henry Hastings, Lord Loughborough. It surrendered in 1646 and two years later the fortifications were demolished. Some surviving residential buildings were later incorporated within a new house called Ashby Place, which was demolished in 1830.

Ashby Castle became a popular tourist resort in the 19th century, in part through its mention in Sir Walter Scott's novel *Ivanhoe* (1819). Kirby remained little-known until it was cleared and repaired by the Ministry of Works between 1911 and 1913.

Above: A portrait of Edward IV (r. 1461–3), the patron and friend of William, Lord Hastings

Facing page: The doorway to the great chamber in the great tower at Ashby. The landing is decorated with the heraldry of the Hastings family. The stone bench on the staircase is probably a 19th-century addition

Tour of Ashby de la Zouch Castle

From the ticket office it is possible to appreciate the layout of Ashby de la Zouch Castle. The cluster of ruined buildings dominated by the kitchen tower and great tower formed the core of the residence. The large lawn with prominent earthworks is the remains of a garden. The approach to the castle was originally through a lost outer court, later the site of Ashby Place, which lay towards the town and parish church to the left. A new house was built on that site in 1831 to 1832. It is now a school and closed to the public.

FOLLOWING THE TOUR

The tour takes in the remains of the residential and service buildings, and the chapel, before exploring the remains of the gardens. The numbers beside the headings correspond with the small numbered plans in the margins.

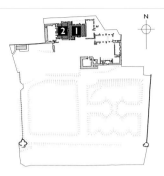

1 HALL

Among the ruins beyond the kitchen tower to the left stands the roofless shell of the hall, the former entrance chamber of the castle apartments. This was the principal public interior of the house, where the Hastings household would have dined.

In their present form, the hall ruins reflect the arrangement of the interior in the 17th century. Probably after the Civil War, the medieval windows were replaced and a fireplace was inserted in one wall. At the same time, the walls were raised in height, which must also have necessitated reroofing the building. This roof survived until the mid-18th century. Early engravings show that it supported a louvre for releasing smoke from the hall fire. In 1645 the repeated arms of Francis Hastings (d.1560) were recorded in the stained glass of the hall windows.

The medieval hall from which this spacious 17th-century interior was created looked very different. It was divided internally by two arcades of arches that sprang from the richly carved capitals that can be seen in the end walls of the room. Set at different levels today, the far pair of capitals were perhaps moved to accommodate the 17th-century roof. The hall was heated by a central hearth, now covered over but visible as a rectangular mound in the middle of the room. Visible in the lawn beyond the hearth are the grassed-over remains of a dais. The high table, where the head of the household could dine with guests, stood on the dais. Tables for the Hastings household would have been ranged along the length of the hall. This building was essentially the 15th-century creation of Lord Hastings, but the two end walls seem to incorporate earlier masonry.

At the other end of the hall to the dais, a pair of porches was added on opposite sides of the medieval building in the 16th century. The principal porch facing the outer court on the far (north) side of the hall preserves the remains of carved decoration and heraldry on its exterior. The internal porch doors were separated from the body of the hall by a timber screen, the stone foundations of which survive.

2 SERVICES

Passing through the pair of doors at the end of the hall, the visitor enters the ruins of what was formerly a two-storey range. At ground level were the buttery and pantry, where beer and bread respectively were stored. A passage running towards the kitchen tower beyond divided the two. The large grid window surviving in one gable wall lit the upper chamber, which was probably a comfortable withdrawing room.

The sunken area of lawn between this building and the kitchen tower was a narrow yard, entered from the outer court to the right (north) through a broad archway. The arch was later narrowed to create a window. Above the arch was

Below: The outer porch to the hall. It was built in the 16th century and the remains of fine neoclassical carving can be seen

Facing page: Detail of a 19th-century engraving by James Pedley of a surviving interior in the north-west angle of the great tower, now inaccessible. The architectural details of the interior, with its fine vault, are correct, but the figure is disproportionately small

Above: The hall (right) and kitchen tower (left). Between the two are the service yard and the ruins of the buttery and pantry

Below: The interior of the kitchen tower showing the scars of the vault

an accounting room, perhaps the 'thoroughfare chamber' mentioned in a document of 1611. Here a clerk could oversee the delivery of provisions to the kitchen and also the marshalling of servants as they prepared to carry cooked food into the hall.

3 KITCHEN TOWER

The scale of the kitchen tower reflects the size of Lord Hastings's household. Its lower two storeys originally formed a vast, vaulted space ringed with hearths and cauldron stands. The cooking space would have been sufficient for a royal palace. Only two hearths remain intact following the demolition of one wall of the tower in 1648 and both were awkwardly repaired in the 19th century. Each originally comprised a hearth for roasting and a stone cauldron stand beside it, lit by a little window. One fireplace also contains the remains of an oven.

The kitchen had its own well, set in a wall niche. A door in the kitchen leads to a 15th-century cellar under the tower with niches for the storage of barrels. Cut through from

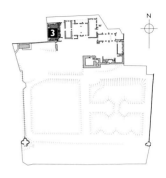

this, probably as part of the Civil War defences, is a tunnel that leads to the great tower. Above the kitchen was a spacious room with large windows, a timber floor and its own latrines. Heated by the kitchen fires, this was quite possibly a winter parlour.

As in a modern restaurant, the kitchen staff was divided into teams, each with its own responsibilities. Food was provided to the household with strict regard for rank, its quantity and quality reflecting the status of the person to whom it was served. As a result, a great variety of dishes would have been prepared here on a regular basis. The staple diet of the household was salted meat, softened with boiling water in cauldrons fixed within the surviving stone stands. Junior members of the kitchen staff may well have slept in this room at night and would have risen early to prepare breakfast. Lord Hastings probably had his own food prepared in the kitchen within the great tower.

Cooked food was passed from the kitchen through the surviving broad hatch into the yard beyond. Sockets for the lost hatch shutter are visible in the masonry. Because food was a valuable commodity, this hatch could be observed through a small window from an office with a fire. From here, an official could count dishes on their way to the hall. The peculiar form of the hatch made his task easier: it required a man to stand in the space within the depth of the wall and pass dishes one by one from the kitchen to the yard.

To either side of the kitchen tower there were further service ranges. The ornamented roofline of the south range is clearly visible in the tower masonry.

Above: A cauldron stand within a fireplace in the kitchen. It is lit from behind by its own small window
Left: A reconstruction of the interior of the kitchen in the 15th century. Even by the standards of medieval kitchens, this was unusually large. The high vault was decorated with carved bosses of stone, a rare ornament in a kitchen. Each of the fireplaces originally incorporated several cooking spaces, such as cauldron stands for boiling, fireplaces for roasting and ovens for baking

Above: The 15th-century fireplace of the great chamber. Its overmantel is carved with the figures of angels and shields

Right: The remains of fireplaces and doorways from a two-storey residential range in the inner court. The large culvert on the right drained the inner court and also the latrine hidden in the thickness of the wall

Below: Panels of 16th-century heraldic glass in the parish church. Some of this glass may originally have been in the chapel

◢ GREAT CHAMBER

At the opposite end of the hall from the services is a pair of withdrawing apartments, probably a parlour at ground level with a great chamber above. These were the principal entertaining rooms for important guests. The great chamber preserves its fine 15th-century fireplace and a huge grid window, cut through in the 16th century.

An inventory of 1596 records that the great chamber was hung with tapestries depicting 'the story of the Romans', besides several carpets, chairs, a chest and bedding. There were also fire irons and a warming pan. It is possible that the parlour was known as the 'bull's head chamber', after the Hastings family crest.

A two-storey range, of which only a chimney stack remains, opened off the great chamber, towards the outer court. This was probably a 16th-century lodging range for senior members of the household. There was also a small room, now lost, with windows on to the chapel for viewing the Mass.

◪ CHAPEL

Lord Hastings built the chapel, which would have been served by priests and singers from his household when he was in residence. They sat in stalls along the sides. The high altar, backed by a painted or sculpted altarpiece, was on a dais at the far end. In 1907 the eastern part of the chapel was screened off for use as a burial place for the Hastings family.

Scars and sockets in the walls show that there were two balconies, one above the other, within the western end. The family or senior servants could observe the service in private from these so-called closets. The first-floor closet was connected to the great chamber by a door, now bricked up.

After the Reformation, the Hastings family became Protestant and employed many notable radical preachers. The religious imagery in the chapel was probably destroyed at this time. Sixteenth-century panelling at Smisby parish church is reputedly from Ashby de la Zouch.

6 INNER COURT

The chapel, great tower and curtain wall enclosed a small courtyard of buildings. The marks of a roofline and wall sockets for timbers of a lost range are clearly visible against the blank, south wall of the chapel. The 1596 inventory shows that this courtyard contained bedchambers and a great parlour, which was perhaps connected to the great chamber by a first-floor gallery. Several of these rooms are described as overlooking the garden.

In the 15th-century outer wall are several medieval fireplaces, many with fixings for different types of fire irons. The large culvert drained the courtyard and also the latrine hidden within the thickness of the wall.

A long tunnel connecting this range to a triangular building called the Mount, on the rise beyond the castle, is reliably documented. The tunnel was probably dug during the Civil War for the movement of troops around the defences. It appears to have been destroyed in the 20th century during the construction of buildings to the east of the castle. The Mount is privately owned and not accessible to the public.

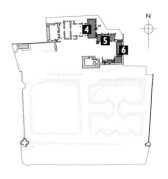

Below: The central panel of an altarpiece by Hans Memling (d.1494), which was probably created for use in a private chapel. The kneeling woman on the right is Elizabeth, the sister of Lord Hastings

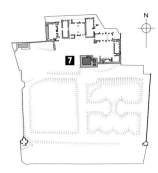

⁊ GREAT TOWER

The great tower was the architectural centrepiece of the castle and, even as a ruin, remains an eloquent testament to the power and wealth of Lord Hastings. Its small entrance door is ornamented with the lions of England, now much worn. It could be secured with a portcullis that fitted within the grooves on each side of the opening. High above the door in an ornamented niche are the heraldic 'achievements' of Lord Hastings: his arms, helm, crest and supporters. The Hastings coat of arms appears in several other places on the outside of the tower.

The tower was crowned by a projecting parapet of battlements and elegantly panelled turrets at the corners, the remains of which survive. It is built of cut stone and its windows grow in scale and grandeur on each floor, a reflection of the relative importance of the rooms inside.

Above: The great tower from the gardens. It was demolished in 1648, probably with gunpowder. For a key to the rooms in the tower, see the cutaway drawing on the facing page

Below left: The doorway of the great tower is ornamented with the worn sculpture of lions, representing the king of England, and foliage

Below centre: The fireplace of the great chamber is decorated with Edward IV's heraldic symbol of sunbursts

Below right: A detail of the remains of the kitchen vault

CUTAWAY OF THE GREAT TOWER IN ABOUT 1480

1 Great chamber, where William, Lord Hastings, would have received guests. The room was hung with tapestries

2 Parlour or withdrawing chamber

3 Kitchen

4 Basement for storage

5 Entrance passage

6 Treasure chamber, accessible only by ladder

7 Withdrawing chamber, possibly Lord Hastings's study

Above: A detail of the arms of Hastings on the great tower showing the maunch, or sleeve. The black inlay may be bitumen
Right: The imposing inner face of the great tower. The tiny entrance is emphasized by the projecting strip of stone and the heraldic 'achievements' above
Below: The Hastings 'achievements' over the entrance to the great tower

The arrangement of the rooms is best understood from the ruined, garden side of the building. There were originally four principal floors in the tower: a basement, a kitchen (both vaulted in stone) and two splendid apartments above. The uppermost preserves a large fireplace with heraldic decoration and – in the left angle of the chamber below it – there is a fine vaulted chamber in the thickness of the wall, now inaccessible (see page 4). Adjoining the main body of the tower is a turret of seven floors. Most of the turret rooms connected to the principal chambers. The room on the first floor, however, has no obvious means of access and was almost certainly a treasure chamber, reached through a trapdoor in the room above. A stack of latrines in the turret served all the floors of the building.

The main stair is set at the juncture of the tower and turret. On the uppermost floor this stairwell is decorated with three carved shields displaying the arms of Hastings, his wife, Katherine, and his son, Edward, and a finely moulded door. From the top of the building is an excellent view of the wider setting of the castle, including the former outer court and gardens. According to the 1596 inventory, the tower kitchen with its fireproof vault was serving as a wardrobe and contained many valuables, including rich fabrics and furniture.

8 GARDEN

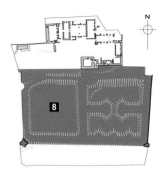

In the mown lawn beyond the great tower are the clear earthwork remains of part of the castle gardens. This unusual survival has been the subject of research and limited archaeological excavation by English Heritage in 2006.

There is record of gardens and orchards at Ashby de la Zouch from the 14th century onwards. In the 1460s, before Lord Hastings started building here, there is reference to 'the great gardens near the manor'. Nothing is known about these. The existing garden remains probably date from about 1530.

The rectangular garden is divided in two by a raised walkway. One half is a broad, level lawn; the other is subdivided by high banks of earth with interlocking spurs. It is possible that the earthwork spurs evoked contemporary bastion fortifications designed for artillery. Some garden designers are known also to have built fortifications, both tasks requiring an ability to move and shape earth. Moreover, fortifications had a strong appeal for the 16th-century English nobility, who continued to view themselves as a professional fighting class.

At the outer corners of the garden are the remains of two brick towers. One to the south-east is polygonal with a projecting stair turret. The other to the south-west is like a four-leafed clover. One of its lobes contains the remains of a staircase and fragments of a fine pavement in the basement. These buildings were probably banqueting houses, where parties of guest could be entertained. In 1596 the building in

Below: A reconstruction of the inner garden of Ashby in about 1630. It shows the position of the round tower revealed by recent excavations

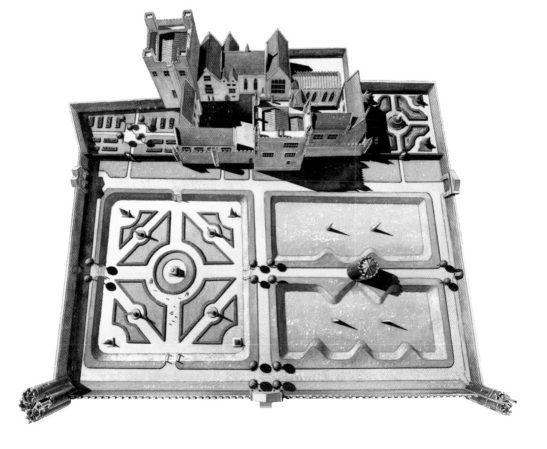

Right: A 19th-century view of the octagonal south-east garden tower before its partial collapse

Facing page: The south-west garden tower is laid out on a clover-leaf plan. It was probably built in about 1540 and compares to the banqueting houses at Hampton Court built by Henry VIII in 1538

the east contained three stills for refining spirits. The large, outward-facing windows of the upper chambers must have offered superb views over the gardens and parkland. A restored external door in the larger tower provided a link between the garden and the wider landscape.

The bedrock lies close to the surface of the garden, making it laborious to level. In the level western half of the garden, excavations revealed a surface incorporating four different colours of roughly compacted stone fragments. These may be the remains of patterns laid in coloured gravel or stone depicting heraldic or geometric designs. The patterns would have been clearly legible from the great tower or the raised walkway along the axis of the garden.

At the centre of the other half of the garden, excavations revealed a third garden tower. This was circular and built of brick identical to that in the corner towers. A staircase gave access from the banks to the sunken areas beneath. It is not clear how this area was planted in the 16th century, though traces of 19th-century garden beds were found.

Enclosing the whole area was a brick wall with a shallow, external ditch. One stretch of the wall with niches for beehives (now blocked) survives beside the kitchen tower.

Above: A map of Ashby in 1735.
It shows the remains of the former
garden compartments as lines of
trees. The Little Park is marked to
the left. The ponds marked 'Moats'
may also have been ornamental
features within the 17th-century
gardens. The triangular Mount
is visible in red towards
the bottom right

THE WIDER LANDSCAPE

The rectangular garden is the surviving element of a much
larger planned landscape created for recreation. A map of
1735, above, reveals the ghosted outlines of nine garden
'compartments' around the castle, and pools beyond. The
compartments would have been planted in contrasting styles
to lend the garden variety. Each probably had a visual focus,
such as a sundial, a statue or a pattern called a knot.

By 1615 the gardens at Ashby also included a 'wilderness',
a newly fashionable type of shady garden planted with trees.
A gate to this was built by a certain Edward Woodcock and
painted in 1616 by a man named Sawyer. The remains of this
gate possibly survive on the public path called Mount Walk to
the east of the castle.

It could have been in this period that a triangular lodge
called the Mount – now a private house – was built on the rise
in another garden compartment overlooking the castle. This
has long been described as a Civil War battery. But, though
the fortifications probably did make use of this structure and
that of the parish church, it probably predates the 1640s.

Three parks extended beyond the gardens. In 1677 the
antiquarian Sir William Dugdale (1605–86) listed them as:
'… the great park, which was ten miles in compass, Bristop
Park for fallow deer; and the Little Park, on the backside of
the house, for red deer'.

The gardens largely disappeared after the Civil War,
though a kitchen garden was maintained until the 18th
century to serve Ashby Place. The wilderness also survived as
a name, which came to be applied to the whole area of the
former gardens around the castle. Only in the 19th century
were the ruins and their surrounds again formally planted.

The Visit of the Countess of Derby

In August 1607, the highly cultivated dowager countess of Derby was welcomed at Ashby by her son-in-law and daughter, the earl and countess of Huntingdon. She was entertained with a theatrical performance in verse written by the playwright John Marston. The text is full of flattery and classical allusions, but the spectacle must have been captivating.

As Lady Derby approached through the Little Park to the sound of trumpets, a gateway was suddenly erected in her path. In front of this there appeared an 'old enchantress in crimson velvet, with pale face, black hair and disliking countenance', who explained that Saturn (representing melancholy) reigned in the house. A guest had lately been expected here, she went on, but winter had barred her passage and everyone was dejected. At that moment, Saturn himself appeared at the gate and recognized the countess as the long-missed guest. Following this recognition, the tone of her reception changed to one of celebration. The countess was then greeted at the top of the stairs to the great chamber by the enchantress – now dressed in white – who, to the sound of music, proclaimed the transformation her arrival had caused. She then presented the countess with a splendid waistcoat.

Later Lady Derby was entertained in the great chamber. Cynthia (the moon) appeared dressed in blue silk riding on a cloud that rose to the ceiling of the room and sank again. She was joined by Ariadne (a figure supposedly crowned by a constellation of stars), and together they determined to visit the beautiful and virtuous ladies they saw in the audience. Ariadne lamented the absence of her crown of stars but, after a song, a curtain fell to reveal her constellation (in the form of eight men), who then danced with the women in the room. A shepherd concluded the performance with a lament that Lady Derby had to leave the house.

> Saturn himself appeared at the gate and recognized the countess as the long-missed guest

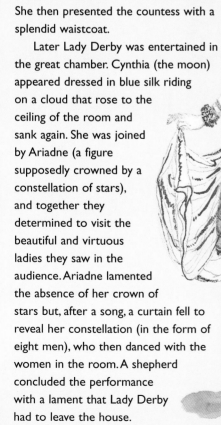

Below: A design of about 1605 for a winged masque costume by Inigo Jones

Tour of Kirby Muxloe Castle

Lord Hastings began to rebuild his family seat at Kirby Muxloe in the most sumptuous fashion in October 1480. After his execution in June 1483, his widow Katherine continued the work on a much reduced scale until the following summer. Although the huge sum of about one thousand pounds was spent on the buildings over this time, the castle was left unfinished. What survives are the incomplete and ruined remains of an ambitiously conceived moated courtyard residence entered through a great gatehouse. It was built on the site of an earlier manor house, of which fragments remain.

OVERVIEW

The surviving courtyard of Lord Hastings's new residence was laid out on a rectangular plan. It was regularly planned with a tower at each corner, one of which still stands to its full height. The double circuit of walls would have formed a spectacular array of battlements: a tall inner wall and a low apron wall along the edge of the moat.

It is unclear how the domestic buildings within these walls were to be arranged. They may have been intended to stand against the inner wall to create a central courtyard or the intention may have been to form several smaller courts inside the moated area, with the hall, great chamber and other residential buildings clustered together around one, as is known in other mid-15th-century sites such as Rye House in Hertfordshire.

Lord Hastings's new buildings at Kirby were made of locally manufactured brick, with details such as windows and doors in stone, a combination of materials fashionable in England at the time and one, moreover, familiar to the master mason of Kirby Muxloe, John Cowper. Cowper trained from 1453 as an apprentice in the building of Eton College, where the English tradition of fine brickwork was effectively founded. Several architectural ideas that developed at Eton – including the combined use of brick and stone – were to prove vastly influential.

Another distinctive feature of the masonry at Kirby, also found at Eton, are the patterns of dark bricks laid into the walls, a method of decoration termed 'diaper'. Among the devices depicted in this unusually elaborate display at Kirby are intersecting diagonal hatching as well as the initials 'WH'

Below: An aerial view of Kirby from the north-west. The rectangular plan, with the projections at each corner for the intended four towers, can clearly be seen

Facing page: The gatehouse of Kirby Muxloe Castle. The walls incorporate an unusually rich variety of patterns laid in dark bricks, known as diaper work

Above: A picture of a jug depicted in diaper work on the gatehouse. It is not clear why this subject (or many others, such as the ship) was chosen
Below: Kirby Muxloe in about 1906. Restoration work a few years later stripped away all traces of its years of use as a farmyard

for William Hastings, the sleeve, or 'maunch', from his coat of arms, a ship and a jug. The diaper decoration is explicitly referred to in the surviving building accounts, which make references to the payments for creation of 'pictures' in the walls. The fact that these payments are only occasional may suggest that the diaper was applied as cosmetic decoration to the surface of the wall.

EARLIER BUILDINGS

The residence that existed at Kirby before 1480 was laid out around two courts, a relatively conventional medieval arrangement. The principal domestic buildings probably stood within the moated site of the present castle; the broken lines of their stone foundations – tentatively identified as belonging to a hall and its associated chamber and service block – are clearly visible in the lawn. These buildings were preserved and even repaired during the Hastings's 1480s rebuilding work, but the intention was presumably to demolish and replace them as his new residence advanced. As this work was never completed they may well have continued in use until the abandonment of the site, probably in the 17th century.

It is likely that the outer court of the original residence lay beyond the present gatehouse in the area now occupied by the carpark and pub. Nothing is securely known of the buildings it contained, although castles and manor houses commonly possessed an outer or base court for ancillary and service buildings such as barns and stables. It is almost certain, therefore, that Lord Hastings intended to preserve this court or even augment it in his redevelopment of the site. The building accounts also mention the clearance of a garden, which may have lain adjacent to the base court.

Kirby Castle.

Left: The remains of the medieval bridge as it was revealed in 1911 to 1913

Below: A farm cart can be seen through the door of the entrance to the gatehouse, drawn by J Blower in about 1840, when Kirby was being used as a farmyard

KIRBY MUXLOE TODAY

As it stands today, Kirby is largely the creation of a 1911 to 1913 restoration which stripped away the later accretions (it had served for many years as a farmyard). Very little was found during the excavations at this time, as any useful building material had been removed over the centuries. The foundations discovered were then consolidated. The moat was re-cut and the remains of a medieval timber bridge leading to the gatehouse revealed. A replica bridge was built to give access to the castle. This was repaired in 2006 during an extensive restoration programme when much of the brickwork of the main buildings was replaced.

GATEHOUSE

Entrance to the inner court was via a colossal new gatehouse, the base of which remains. According to the accounts, work to the gatehouse began in about June 1482. The building was probably abandoned in much its present state two years later. If the intended dimensions of the gatehouse were a proportionate enlargement of those found on the surviving corner tower, it would have stood more than 30m tall (or about 100ft, a symbolic benchmark height for medieval skyscrapers). In plan the building is rectangular with a polygonal turret at each corner, a relatively common design at this date. The turrets to the rear both incorporate a spiral stair. To either side of the main front there are projecting rectangular turrets that house latrines.

A much later building that echoes the distinctive plan of the gatehouse and which may give an insight into its intended final form is the great gate of Layer Marney, Essex. Begun in the 1520s by Henry, Lord Marney (d.1523), this immensely tall

structure of eight storeys also belongs to a house that was apparently never completed.

The gatehouse was approached across a wooden bridge with a drawbridge at one end. Timbers from the original bridge are preserved in the bed of the moat. The drawbridge mechanism was located in the first-floor room of the gatehouse. There are holes for the ropes or chains that operated it at each upper corner of the shallow recess around the archway, which was designed to house the drawbridge when it was raised.

Above the gateway is an empty rectangular niche ornamented with a foliage border, almost certainly the frame for a sculpted panel of Lord Hastings's heraldic achievements. He is further celebrated in the diaper decoration around the gate, which includes his initials WH and his emblem, the maunch. The mouth of the gate passage was closed by a portcullis (now lost), which fitted in a deep groove within the door frame, and a gate. The present gate incorporates some timbers from its medieval predecessor.

All the gatehouse ground-floor chambers were vaulted in brick. Unfortunately, the gate passage vault, which may have been splendidly decorated, does not survive. The others are featureless domes or barrels.

Below: One of the spiral stairways of the gatehouse

To either side of the gate passage is a chamber lit by a fire. That to the right of the entrance was probably the porter's lodge. It has a large window overlooking the passage, which permitted the porter to monitor the castle entrance.

Opening through the outer walls of the ground-floor rooms are numerous gun loops. These take the form of a small circular opening for the muzzle of the gun and a vertical slit above for aiming it. Below the moat waterline in the gatehouse there survives a series of canon loops. These had to be blocked because they were built too low – a curious instance of a medieval mason's error.

The first floor of the gatehouse, from where the portcullis and drawbridge were worked, can be reached by both the spiral stairways to the rear of the building. This double system of access as well as the scale of the room may suggest that it was intended for ceremonial rather than domestic use. It was luxuriously appointed, with two fires, latrines and large windows. The lines of sockets in the window frames are the fixings for iron stanchions, or grilles.

There was another storey above it which no longer exists and may never have been finished. The latrine chamber on the first floor of the north turret was at some point made into a pigeon house.

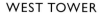

WEST TOWER

Six further towers were intended at the angles and mid-points of the perimeter wall of the inner court. Surviving foundations or small rectangular platforms projecting into the moat indicate the positions of five of these. Only the west tower survives as a complete structure, and is the best preserved part of the castle. The brick toothings for the north-west range that would have joined the tower to the gatehouse are still visible.

The west tower is square in plan and comprises three floors, the lower ringed by six gun loops. There is also a loop on the north-east side of the stair turret commanding the rampart walk. The small diameter of the openings must have limited the field of fire. Rising up the two inner faces of the tower are two turrets. One contains a spiral staircase and the other a stack of latrines serving each floor. The rooms within the tower were probably intended as lodging chambers for senior members of Lord Hastings's household. The wall tops are embattled, with stone copings. At parapet level the tower preserves two fine octagonal brick chimneys. The patterned brickwork of this tower is simpler than that of the gatehouse.

ACCOUNTING FOR THE WORK

Much of what we know about Kirby Muxloe Castle is derived from a surviving set of building accounts covering the period 1480 to 1484. These were compiled by Lord Hastings's steward, Roger Bowlott, and are written on sheets of paper bound up as a small book about 30cm x 20cm (12in x 8in) in size. The language is a mixture of Latin, French and English: it records, for example, buying 'iiij pecie meremii vocate le polles pro iiij Corneriis pro levelyng le ertha infra muros', meaning 'four pieces of timber called poles for the four corners for levelling the earth within the walls'. Charted in this volume is a week-by-week account of the progress of works, providing a fascinating insight into the daily operation of a medieval building site.

Work was accounted from the week beginning 23 October 1480, at which time supplies were being delivered to the 'brick house', presumably to start the large-scale manufacture of bricks necessary for the forthcoming project. This was under the supervision of a Fleming, Antony Yzebrond, who was paid a weekly 10*d*. When production of bricks properly got underway, 100,000 were being burned in a week. At the start of operations a man called John Powell was redirecting a brook to feed the moat and a workman, Hugh Geffrey, was building a cart track for the carriage of stone. A week later oak and ash trees were being uprooted to create a garden beside the new castle. It was presumably for planting in this garden that a certain John Peyntour was sent out in December to gather crab apple trees as grafting stock.

Above: Brickmakers at work shaping, stacking to dry, and burning bricks, depicted in a 15th-century Flemish Bible

After a winter lull, activity on the site rapidly intensified and from 26 February 1481 the accounts adopt a new format. Henceforth – and in conventional fashion for the period – each category of expense within them is independently listed. So, for example, that week there are itemised payments to labourers, gardeners, carters and ditchers. Then, on 7 May, there arrive freemasons, roughmasons, servants of the said masons and bricklayers.

Leading this group is a 'mastermason, surveyor over the stone-masons there', later identified as John Cowper. Confusingly, at this time he was based at Tattershall in Lincolnshire, where he was employed in completing the collegiate church for William Waynflete, bishop of Winchester. The terms of his employment at Kirby are unclear, but the accounts show that he received 10 shillings for every occasion he was called to the site and four shillings a week while he remained there. In June 1481 he also received a bed by prior agreement.

The accounts chart the medieval building cycle, with lulls in activity every winter enforced by the cold weather, when walls were covered with stubble or straw to protect them from frost and the wages of the men declined. Work continued at a relatively brisk pace until Lord Hastings's death, after which time expenditure dropped sharply. The number of men employed on site seems to have varied greatly. In the first week of work in October 1480 there were just 17 men present, but during the height of works there were regularly over 40 men working on the ditching and building.

From the clerk's terse entries it can be difficult to unpick the course of the project. So, for example, in March 1482, what are described as the 'basse tours' and 'mydultours' were being demolished. A month later, the same 'base towers' and 'middle towers' were being re-erected. Were the demolished buildings part of the old residence or had the masons built something incorrectly? We will never know. Mentioned in the accounts are many buildings of which no trace today remains, including a kitchen, an oxhouse and a great chamber. One curiosity they also describe is an engine or 'ginne' erected on one of the towers to raise building materials.

It is clear from the accounts that at least one tower (presumably the west corner tower) was nearly finished in 1483 and that the ground floor of the gatehouse with its entrance vault was complete. Of the wider state of the site, little can be securely deduced from this surviving documentary evidence.

Above: Builders using a crane to construct a tower in about 1500. A similar 'ginne', or engine, used to lift building materials is listed in the accounts of the 1480s at Kirby Muxloe

Left: The great tower of Tattershall Castle in Lincolnshire was built in the 1440s. It was known to John Cowper and may have served as a model for the gatehouse at Kirby Muxloe

History

Ashby de la Zouch Castle has enjoyed an unusually varied history. Together with Kirby Muxloe Castle it was developed on a grand scale by William, Lord Hastings, favourite of Edward IV. After his execution in 1483 it became the seat of the Hastings family. The castle was besieged in the Civil War and partially demolished. The ruins were subsequently repaired and the site reoccupied. In the 19th century, Ashby became a tourist destination thanks to its inclusion in a bestselling novel.

WILLIAM, LORD HASTINGS

At Nottingham on 17 April 1474, William, Lord Hastings, the chamberlain of England, received a licence from Edward IV to fortify with walls and battlements four manor houses within his great estates: Ashby de la Zouch, Bagworth (with Thornton) and Kirby Muxloe, all in Leicestershire, and Slingsby in Yorkshire. The licence also permitted him to enclose up to 9,000 acres of land around these buildings to create hunting parks. The right to hunt and the ownership of castles or houses fortified with towers and battlements were the distinguishing marks of nobility. With this licence, Lord Hastings was assuming on a grand scale the trappings of wealth and political power. His spectacular rebuilding of Ashby, an obscure manor house confiscated from his recently conquered Lancastrian enemies, was designed to show clearly that the balance of power had changed in the Midlands and that he now controlled the region.

William Hastings was born in about 1430. His father, Sir Leonard Hastings (d.1455) of Kirby Muxloe, had served the duke of York in the dynastic struggle for the throne known as the Wars of the Roses. William assumed his father's allegiance to the house of York, and was knighted on the battlefield of Towton, north Yorkshire, in 1461 by the duke of York's son and heir, Edward IV. William Hastings enjoyed further privileges from the king. He was summoned to parliament as Baron Hastings in July 1461 and the next month appointed chamberlain of the royal household. Between 1462 and 1464, he also acquired blocks of land in his native Midlands and beyond, much of it confiscated from Edward IV's opponents. Among these was the ancient and valuable manor of Ashby.

ASHBY BEFORE THE CASTLE

The manor of Ascebi is first documented in the Domesday survey of 1086 and for the next century formed part of the estates of the earls of Leicester. The earls granted it to a family of Breton descent with the name 'le Zouch' (meaning 'a stock' or 'stem') in return for military service. This family held the property for more than two centuries and gave the town its name. Their manor house probably stood on the site of the present castle but it was not an important or splendid residence. A description of 1347 records 'a ruinous old hall, a new chamber not yet roofed … and a long house called the bakery, brewhouse and kitchen'. There was also a well, an oast house, a dovecote, an orchard and a warren. Fragments of these buildings are possibly preserved in the hall range.

The death of the last direct heir to the Zouch inheritance in 1399 initiated a protracted dispute over the ownership of Ashby, which was resolved only in 1467. Effective control of the manor had passed by 1461 to the prominent Lancastrian James Butler, earl of Ormond and earl of Wiltshire. He was executed after

Above: Richard Plantagenet, duke of York, whom William Hastings's father served during the Wars of the Roses; a 19th-century engraving of a statue that used to stand on Welsh Bridge, Shrewsbury

Facing page: A marginal illustration from the Hastings hours showing the family arms. Its naturalistic borders are distinctive of the most sophisticated manuscripts from Bruges and Ghent in the late 15th century. Lord Hastings, exiled with Edward IV at the Burgundian court in the Low Countries, introduced many of its splendours to England

deo placiuisti. Egenos et hos
bisos de abo foiuisti. Cecos
multos debiles et claudos i
uisti. Semper elemosinam
dare quesiuisti. Deum et
ecclesiam virgo dilexisti
fraudem et nequiciam tu
inime odisti. Para nobis
gloriam quam tu meruisti

Above: William, Lord Hastings, was a skilled and enthusiastic jouster. This is a page from the Hastings hours, commissioned by Lord Hastings in the Low Countries in about 1480. The manuscript may well have been used by him in the closet in the chapel at Ashby

the battle of Towton and his estate declared forfeit.

Ashby was part of a large grant of land made to William, Lord Hastings, on 17 February 1462, but there is no evidence that he favoured Ashby at first. This situation changed when Edward IV was briefly deposed in 1470–71 by the earl of Warwick, known as 'the kingmaker'. Lord Hastings fled with Edward IV to the Low Countries and at Bruges plotted a return to power. On 14 March 1471 Edward IV and his supporters landed at Ravenspur on the Humber estuary. Lord Hastings provided the first important complement of men for his army, mustering 3,000 supporters at Leicester.

When Edward IV once again established himself on the throne, Lord Hastings began to enjoy much greater powers. A combination of royal appointments and private agreements with individuals and institutions made him a virtual vice-regent in Derbyshire, Nottinghamshire, Leicestershire and parts of Warwickshire. He was courted for his influence; as a servant of the Paston family reported in 1472, he could do more with the king 'than any man alive'. The duke of Burgundy bought his favour with a princely annuity of 1,000 ecus in 1471 and four years later the French king offered him a pension of 2,000 gold crowns. Remarkably for so successful a courtier, he was respected and liked by many of his rivals.

THE BUILDING OF THE CASTLE

The 1474 licence to fortify four manors and create parks around them was a public statement of Lord Hastings's intention to celebrate his new status. It does not date the works it describes. The first reference at Ashby to 'diverse great works within the manor and the wages of carpenters, tillers, masons, plumbers and other artificers and their servants' occurs in manorial roll for 1472–3, a full year before the licence was issued. The building accounts of Kirby show that work here began only in 1480.

It is clear that Lord Hastings intended Ashby de la Zouch to serve as his principal seat. This was indicated by the great tower that still dominates the site. Huge, rectangular towers were a feature of most major English castles since the 11th century, and by building one at Ashby Lord Hastings was making his new residence the architectural equal of the most ancient and important castles in the kingdom. The form and details of this building were almost certainly related to those of the great towers built at the royal castles of Tutbury (1460s) and Nottingham (from 1476). They also resemble those of the great gatehouse at Farnham Castle, built in the 1470s by the bishop of Winchester.

Lord Hastings also built the kitchen tower, probably as part of a coherent rebuilding plan. Indeed, as Dugdale observed in 1677, despite their differences in detail, the two towers are 'as it should seem, and as by tradition it hath been told, built in such a figure, that two more might be placed at convenient distance to equal them.' The idea of Ashby as a regularly planned castle with four towers set around its perimeter wall is breathtaking in its ambition, and does indeed match the surviving evidence. At the same time, the existing manor house was remodelled and expanded, with a new chapel and service buildings. Lord Hastings was a discerning patron and the buildings he created reflect the sophistication of life in his household. As royal chamberlain, responsible for the running of the household, he introduced to England the protocol of the Burgundian court, the richest and most admired in contemporary Europe.

It is a mark of Lord Hastings's outstanding wealth that work to Kirby was begun in 1480 before the buildings at Ashby were complete. The surviving building accounts record that he employed the important master mason John Cowper in this operation. It is possible that Cowper also designed the great tower at Ashby, though record of the fact is lost.

THE DEATH OF WILLIAM, LORD HASTINGS

The death of Edward IV in 1483 brought the career of Lord Hastings to a dramatic close. An obstacle to the ambitions of the duke of Gloucester, the future Richard III, he was summarily executed on 13 June 1483. Despite having

Above: The 'maunch', or heraldic sleeve, of Hastings picked out in diaper work on the gatehouse at Kirby Muxloe Castle
Below: A portrait of Edward IV in stained glass in Canterbury Cathedral. Visible in the background is the repeated emblem of a rose in a sunburst, Edward IV's badge. The prayer desk he kneels at is decorated with St George and the dragon

Right: A portrait of Elizabeth Woodville. Edward IV's secret marriage to this beautiful but impoverished widow was a great scandal. By introducing her sons to court, she installed the Grey family in the heart of English politics and changed the balance of power in the Midlands

ELIZABETH
EDWARDVS
VXOR
IIII

patronized the burial church of the dukes of Lancaster at St Mary's Newark in Leicester, he was appropriately buried in St George's Chapel, Windsor, begun by his master Edward IV.

This turn of events brought to a close the works at Kirby. Whether the incomplete buildings formed part of a Hastings residence documented at Kirby into the late 17th century is not now clear. By the 18th century, the castle was abandoned and in decay. At Ashby, the revival of his family's fortunes ensured that the residence was not left to ruin.

On 23 July 1483 Richard III issued a special grant to the widow of Lord Hastings, Katherine, restoring the family to its inheritance. The grant was a tacit acknowledgement that the execution had been an act of policy, smoothing Richard's way to the throne. The eldest son, Edward, was still a minor, but entered by stages into his estates from 1487. Edward never commanded the income or power of his father, whose influence had substantially derived from the trust he had enjoyed as a royal servant.

THE HASTINGS FAMILY

Edward did, however, enjoy a brilliant marriage through his father's careful dynastic planning: he obtained the hand of

Mary, daughter and heir of Lord Hungerford. The estates she brought with her bolstered the fortunes of the family in the face of worrying competition. Edward IV's scandalous marriage in 1464 to Elizabeth Woodville, the virtually penniless widow of a local knight, John Grey of Groby, had far-reaching political consequences in the Midlands. Her eldest son, Thomas, was created marquis of Dorset in 1475 and began to build up his position in Leicestershire. Shortly before his death in 1501, he began to rebuild the family seat at Groby Castle, Leicestershire.

Edward Hastings died in 1506 but his formidable widow Mary outlived him by 26 years. Their eldest son, George, had to wait a long time for his considerable maternal inheritance. Meanwhile, Thomas Grey's son, also called Thomas (d.1530), began to expand another nearby residence at Bradgate on the outskirts of Leicester. Such was the competition between the Grey and Hastings families in the region, that an altercation between their servants in Leicester in 1524 escalated into a running battle through the town centre. The next year, in 1525, Thomas Manners was created first earl of Rutland and began to restore Belvoir, a castle that had been reputedly stripped of lead by Lord Hastings to supply the works at Ashby.

In 1529 the family fortunes improved once more when George Hastings was created earl of Huntingdon. The title was almost certainly conferred by Henry VIII as encouragement for George's support in the approaching trial of strength over the royal divorce from Katherine of Aragon. Royal favour brought material rewards. It is likely that George

Left: The chantry of William, Lord Hastings, in St George's Chapel, Windsor. Visible just beyond the chantry is the tomb of Edward IV
Above: The superbly decorated interior of the chantry is vaulted and encloses an altar. One wall is decorated with 15th-century paintings of the life and martyrdom of St Stephen

made important changes to Ashby in brick at about this time in celebration of his title. Certainly, in 1677 Dugdale described the buildings as having formerly been built in a mix of stone and brick. George probably set out the surviving garden with its towers. These might plausibly have been created to match the new gardens laid by his local rivals at both Groby and Belvoir in about 1530.

It was in this improved situation that in 1532 George secured for his eldest son, Francis, the hand of Katherine Pole, a descendant of one of Edward IV's brothers and an heiress. Francis succeeded to the title in 1543 and allied himself to John Dudley, the premier political figure of Edward VI's reign. This alliance was in turn sealed by a marriage between Francis's eldest son, Henry, and Dudley's daughter, Katherine. Curiously, his youngest daughter, Mary, was solicited by the Russian ambassador in London as a bride for Ivan the Terrible. Elizabeth I broke off the suit upon discovering the power that Russian husbands exercised over their wives.

Henry succeeded his father as third earl of Huntingdon in 1560. Through his mother's royal descent, he was viewed as a potential heir to the unmarried and childless Elizabeth I. As a result he was initially treated with hostility by the queen, who was wary of those who might succeed her. So, too, was his wife, who received what is ambiguously described as a 'privy nippe' from Elizabeth. But later the earl came to be trusted as a loyal servant. In the political crisis of 1569 he acted as a gaoler of Mary, queen of Scots, who was briefly held at Ashby

Below: The alabaster tomb of Francis, second earl of Huntingdon (d. 1560), and his wife Katherine Pole in the parish church at Ashby. Francis was described by Edward VI as 'a brave and hardy man, but not over-experienced in war'. Katherine outlived her husband by 16 years. Curiously, the tomb inscription gives an inaccurate date of death for Francis

in November that year. From 1572 he became closely involved in the government of northern England.

Henry died in Yorkshire on 14 December 1595 and his body was transported in state to Ashby for burial according to directions issued by the queen herself. A surviving bill records that the undertaking, including the distribution of black cloth for mourning in London, Coventry, Leicester and Ashby, cost the vast sum of £1,242. An inventory of his goods made in 1596 offers a remarkable picture of the form and furnishing of Ashby before the Civil War.

Henry had run up huge debts in royal service. In 1603–4 his younger brother and heir, George, petitioned James I for relief, claiming liabilities of nearly £30,000 and declaring himself unable to maintain the estate of an earl. Probably in order to further his suit, George angled to secure a royal visit. His solicitations were answered on 22 June 1603, when Queen Anne of Denmark and her son Prince Henry came to the castle. Whether or not this helped George's case is not clear, but his petition was granted by the king in February 1604.

George died in 1605 and was succeeded by his grandson Henry, who also laid on court entertainments, including a day-long reception of James I in 1617 and another for Charles I and Henrietta Maria in 1634. It was probably for such visits that the gardens at Ashby were further developed.

Above left: Henry Hastings, third earl of Huntingdon, by an unknown artist, late 16th-century. Henry was celebrated for his Protestant piety and in 1567 formally endowed a grammar school in Ashby which survives to this day

Top: Anne of Denmark by Isaac Oliver, c.1612. She was entertained at Ashby in 1603 with her son Henry, Prince of Wales, en route from York to London

Above: Henry, Prince of Wales, by Marcus Gheeraerts the Younger, c.1603

Servants and their Duties

When the earl's food was carried to his private dining chamber, the usher called for everyone to stand and doff their hats

Above: Henry, fifth earl of Huntingdon, by Wenceslaus Hollar, mid-17th-century
Below: The Tichborne Dole by Gillis van Tilborch, c.1670. Sir Henry Tichborne distributes bread to the poor. The hierarchy of this large household is expressed in dress

In August 1609, Henry, the fifth earl of Huntingdon, issued at Ashby a set of rules or ordinances for the government of his household. These directions were intended: '… for the better and more exquisite performance of every man's duty in his several place' and they provide a vivid picture of life here in the 17th century.

The ordinances begin with a list of the senior servants and their duties and conclude with a list of the entire household as it was on 20 August 1609. In overall control was the steward. Beneath him were a host of officers responsible for specialist tasks: the clerk of the kitchen administered the purchase of food; the cook oversaw the operation of the kitchen; the gentleman of the horse managed the stable; the yeomen of the pantry, cellar, and buttery respectively supervised measures of bread, wine and beer; the almoner distributed food to the poor, and the porter watched the gate. The usher of the hall was responsible for public ceremonial. When the earl's food was carried to his private dining chamber, for example, the usher called for everyone to stand and doff their hats as it passed through the hall. The household was almost exclusively male and was evidently expected to travel between residences with the earl.

The estimated expenses for running the household for a year are listed as £2,855, which includes £100 for the repair of the earl's houses; £30 for children's clothing; £40 for keeping hawks and hounds; £205 for maintaining stables; £120 for lawsuits; and £560 for the earl and countess's expenses and clothing. By contrast, the wages and clothing for the entire household of 61 gentlefolk and servants cost just £210 per year.

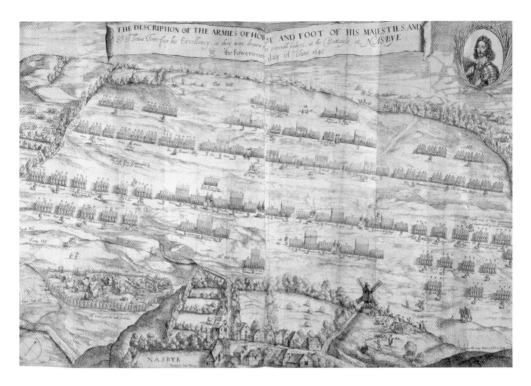

THE CIVIL WAR

At the outbreak of the Civil War, Henry declared his support for Charles I but died in November 1643. His eldest son, Ferdinando, strove to avoid committing himself in the conflict. Ferdinando's younger brother Henry, however, used Ashby as a royalist base and proved an active commander in the Midlands. He was created Lord Loughborough in 1643 and his chief opponent in Leicestershire was the head of the Grey family, who declared for Parliament.

The town and castle at Ashby were fortified by Henry on an impressive scale. To create the defences several houses were demolished and even the grammar school, 'was by the violence of souldiers pulled downe and raced to the ground and all the materials thereof converted to warlike imployment'. The great tower was the focus of these arrangements and described in 1644 as 'Hastings' stronghold'.

Ashby formed a crucial link between royalist operations in the North and South. Charles I twice visited the castle during the fighting in the company of the diarist Colonel Symonds. On the first occasion Symonds was at leisure to record the heraldic glass in the hall. The second visit, however, was brief and unhappy. At Naseby on 14 June 1645 the royalists suffered a decisive and disastrous defeat. Having attended the wounded in Leicester, the king came on to Ashby for the night. When he hurriedly left at about 10am the next day, he can have been in no doubt that his cause was in peril.

The garrison at Ashby was contained by a parliamentarian force that occupied the nearby mansion of Coleorton. An outbreak of plague at Ashby in August 1645 caused a lull in

Top: An engraving of the battle of Naseby, 14 June 1645. Charles I spent the night after this royalist disaster at Ashby, about 30 miles from Naseby
Above: *The seal of the diarist, antiquarian and soldier Richard Symonds. He fought in the king's aristocratic corps, the 'Shew Troop', during the Civil War. In the course of campaigning he visited and recorded monuments, tombs and buildings in his diaries. He ended the war in the garrison at Ashby de la Zouch and after surrendering to Parliament was permitted to leave with two servants on 5 March 1646*

Top: An anonymous oil painting
of the castle at Ashby made
between 1828 and 1830. To the
right are visible the brick remains
of Ashby Place, the house that
developed in the castle ruins.
It was demolished in 1830–1
Above: Selina Hastings, countess of
Huntingdon, c.1770. A flamboyant
young woman who had once
appeared in a dress 'properer for a
stucco staircase than the apparel of
a lady', she became in old age a
religious enthusiast of austere temper

the fighting, but it resumed after the arrival of royalist
reinforcements in November. A series of successful raids on
the town and the king's declining fortunes brought about the
earl's surrender on 28 February 1646. He agreed to demolish
the fortifications around the town. The garrison, meanwhile,
was allowed to march free with ' trumpets sounding, drums
beating, colours flying, matches lighted at both ends, muskets
loaded, one brass gun' and their possessions.

DEMOLITION

By 9 March 1646 the fortifications of Ashby had been levelled.
The triangular Mount House survived, which implies that it
was not built as a fortification. The castle buildings, however,
stood complete and were used to imprison prominent
royalists. In May there was a scare that Henry might reoccupy
the great tower and in November the defences of the
residence were demolished. The earl later complained that the
demolition squad had far exceeded its orders and ruined his
'only convenient mansion'.

But Ashby was not abandoned, although from now on the
earls of Huntingdon used a nearby house at Donington as
their principal residence. The buildings, including the medieval
hall, were patched together as a house called Ashby Place.
Presumably in conjunction with this work (and certainly by
1730) the ruins were cleared of rubble, a massive task. Ashby
Place appears to have been used as a dower house by widowed
countesses of Huntingdon, but little is known of its development.
The house was repaired in 1724, and between 1730 and 1770
the medieval hall was abandoned and lost its roof.

One of the last family occupants of Ashby Place was
Selina, who lived here after the death of her husband, the
ninth earl of Huntingdon, in 1746. She gave over the laundry

– reputedly a garden building put up for the visit of James I – to a nonconformist preacher as a meeting house. In 1783 she founded the Calvinist sect called the Countess of Huntingdon's Connexion. Unlike many nonconformists, Selina supported slavery and owned a plantation in Georgia. She even directed her agents to buy a slave and name her Selina.

ASHBY AND 19TH-CENTURY TOURISM

The last Hastings earl of Huntingdon, Francis, died without children in 1789 and his estates passed by marriage to Francis Rawdon, later earl of Moira. He invested in the Ashby Canal, which opened in 1804 and connected the town with London. Determined to use it to exploit coal reserves on his estate, that year he sank the Moira Mine just outside Ashby. A spring revealed in the mine eventually proved as lucrative as the coal.

In 1819, the novelist Sir Walter Scott published a medieval romance, *Ivanhoe*. A tournament in the novel was set at Ashby and visitors flocked to see the ruins. Francis Rawdon's agent, Edward Mammatt, saw the opportunity to transform Ashby into a spa town. The centrepiece would be the Ivanhoe Baths, which opened in 1822, supplied by water from the Moira Mine. Mammatt appreciated the importance of the castle: he repaired the ruins, transforming them into a popular resort, and the first guidebook to the castle was published in 1824.

Francis Rawdon benefited from the redevelopment of Ashby. As one commentator noted in 1903–7, however, Mammatt, 'while apparently zealous in furthering his Lordship's interests, was careful not to neglect his own'. Ashby Place was now neglected and in use as a House of Industry for poor relief. In 1830, Mammatt's son John got permission from Francis Rawdon to demolish it and build in its place 'Ashby Manor', which survives as a school. Its Gothic design was judged in Pigot's National Commercial Directory of 1835 to be in 'the finest taste exercised successfully in combining the advantages of elegance and comfort'.

Above: Francis Rawdon, later earl of Moira and marquess of Hastings, 1754–1826. He was a noted soldier and imperial administrator
Below: The Ivanhoe Baths, Ashby. They were opened in 1822 as part of a spa development in the town undertaken by Francis Rawdon's agent, Edward Mammatt

Top: Visitors photographed posing in the ruins at Ashby in about 1900
Above: Ivanhoe by Sir Walter Scott. The novel was a huge public success after its first publication in 1819, and catapulted Ashby into the public consciousness. The castle became a popular tourist destination. This edition was published by T Nelson & Sons, London and Edinburgh, in 1901

REDISCOVERY AND RESTORATION

The ruins of the castle became an adjunct to Ashby Manor. Repairs continued throughout the 19th century, focusing on the two towers. Most of the buildings remained covered in ivy but there was limited excavation, probably in about 1900. The results were recorded by a Leicester architect, Thomas Fosbrooke, who published the first accurate surveys of the castle in 1911. By this time antiquarian and archaeological societies also began to make regular visits to the castle.

Kirby Muxloe was also beginning to attract interest. In 1855 it was reported that the late owner, Mr Winstanley, had repaired the ruins, and deprecated his father's decision to demolish a tower to make a barn. In 1911 the castle was placed under state guardianship and over the next two years its fabric was restored by Sir Charles Peers, chief inspector of ancient monuments. He dug out the moat and exposed the remains of the medieval bridge. At this time, the 15th-century building accounts were rediscovered by Thomas Fosbrooke.

In 1926, the Hastings archives were sold to the American railway magnate Henry Huntington, and remain in the Huntington Library in California. Ashby de la Zouch came into state guardianship in 1932 and was cleared by the Ministry of Works before the Second World War. Since 1983 both Ashby and Kirby have been in the care of English Heritage, which continues to research and conserve them. Repairs were undertaken to Kirby in 2005–6 and in 2006 the gardens at Ashby were the subject of excavation and historical research.